IMAGES
of America

TEXAS COUNTY

On the Cover: This photograph is of the Mr. and Mrs. Charles Hitch Rodeo Show. Featured in the picture are Mrs. Henry Hitch and Ladd Hitch on the horses. Also in the picture are Mr. and Mrs. C.R. Miller, Mr. and Mrs. Jim England, Billy Stephens, Mrs. Carl Clawson, Mrs. Red Atkins, Ottis Stephens, Margaret Stephens, Della Hitch Keating, Robert Hitch, Charles Keating, Jim Keating, Ruby Hitch Waters, Lottie Hitch Rainey, and Earnest Stephens. (Charles Dean Miller files.)

Harold Kachel, Pauline Hodges, and Kathal Bales

ISBN 978-1-5316-6131-1

Published by Arcadia Publishing
Charleston, South Carolina

Library of Congress Control Number: 2012949290

For all general information, please contact Arcadia Publishing:
Telephone 843-853-2070
Fax 843-853-0044
E-mail sales@arcadiapublishing.com
For customer service and orders:
Toll-Free 1-888-313-2665

Visit us on the Internet at www.arcadiapublishing.com

This book is dedicated to those courageous ranchers and homesteaders who came to No Man's Land to bring new life and new means of making a living. These hearty and brave folk built new towns, schools, churches, and businesses in order to make a good life for themselves and their descendants. They were able to establish a new county government, organize and develop a state university, bring new enterprises to the area as well as survive the Dust Bowl and hard times of drought and the Great Depression. We are grateful to Dr. Nolan McWhirter, who established the No Man's Land Museum, and to those who have maintained and promoted it in order to record our unique heritage as well as to the No Man's Land Historical Society and those who served on its board of directors for years, such as Bill Baker, Ladd Hitch, Gerald Dixon, Mark Mayo, Stanley Tyler, and many others.

CONTENTS

Acknowledgments

The authors appreciate the use of pictures and stories from the files of Charles Miller of Albuquerque and Gerald Dixon of Guymon, both from pioneer families in Texas County. Their generosity was invaluable in capturing the spirit and history of the early-day folk who braved hard times and difficult conditions to settle an uninhabited land. Other pictures loaned to us include those from Sue Weissinger of the No Man's Land Museum in Goodwell, Oklahoma, in the heart of Texas County. Weissinger gave of her time to find them in the archives of the museum and organize them for the authors' search. In addition, information from Weissinger's book *Cattle, Wheat, and Oil* provided a reliable source to clarify dates and names of early settlements in what would later become Texas County. An invaluable source of information was *The Encyclopedia of Oklahoma History and Culture.* Information from Dr. Sara Richter's book Images of America: *The Panhandle* and Gerald Dixon's book *80 Years of Memories in No Man's Land* were also used to verify facts. Shelley Burgess lent her copy of *Hardesty History,* published by the Hardesty Homemakers Group; as well as her copy of *Ten Decades of Texhoma* and *Pioneer Memorial Picture Book of Iva Elliott,* which were of great help. Our appreciation also goes to the area schools, public libraries, cooperatives, businesses, town halls, and churches for their contributions of pictures and information. Others who contributed information and pictures were Supt. Rex Hale of the Optima School, Joe Lawder, JoDean James, Chris Hitch, Geraldine Latham, Chris Purdy and Stephanie Chapman of Panhandle Telephone Cooperative Inc., Juliann Graham of Tri-County Electric, Shirley Burgess, Diane Ellis, Bernell Richards, Connie Taylor of the Guymon Methodist Church, and Ginger Roach of the Texhoma Museum.

INTRODUCTION

Texas County did not officially exist until the area known as No Man's Land, the Neutral Strip, and later as Cimarron Territory was "tacked on" to Oklahoma Territory in 1890. However, thousands of years before that time, prehistoric peoples had inhabited the area, as evidenced by artifacts found on farms, beside roadbeds, and on the mesas and cliffs along the rivers and creeks in the area. There is evidence that people inhabited the area even before the known Clovis and Folsom peoples in the area, and by evidence along the rivers of a "slab" people who formed structures out of slabs of stone. There is also evidence of prehistoric peoples in the artifacts exhibited in the No Man's Land Museum in Goodwell, Oklahoma, found in the area and possibly even older than these two known earlier cultures. Spear points and axe heads dating back thousands of years have been found along creek beds and riverbeds, pointing to prehistoric cultures not yet fully examined, as well as writings on cave walls indicating people in the area long before written history.

These artifacts found on farms, beside roadbeds, and on mesas and cliffs along the rivers indicate the prehistoric periods that have yet to be fully explored. These tools and weapons of early Native Americans are exhibited in the No Man's Land Museum in Goodwell, where the extensive collection reflects the life here long before Caucasian settlers came. As modern farming methods change, new roads, dams, and ditches are built, and new artifacts turn up frequently. It is apparent that we do not fully know the history of mankind in the area. This book has chapters and pictures that show the discoveries made thus far into that prehistoric era, as indicated by the artifacts, ruins, writings on cave walls, and tools used by prehistoric peoples. The area is rich in these treasures, not only in present-day Texas County but also in the counties in the adjoining states and the adjacent counties in the Panhandle. The area is fortunate to have the No Man's Land Museum, offering an extensive collection of prehistoric bones, spear points, axe heads, and other artifacts of these prehistoric settlers in the area, as well as more recent folk who either came through or settled the area. The museum is fortunate to have been established by Oklahoma Panhandle A&M College, now Oklahoma Panhandle State University, which had a professor attuned to collecting these early artifacts, instituted a museum adjacent to the college, and preserved what was found on farms and ranches through the years. The area is eternally grateful to Dr. Nolan McWhirter for preserving this prehistoric time that would have otherwise been housed in museums hundreds of miles from the area or not kept at all. The entire area, as well as Texas County, was also fortunate to have other professors at Oklahoma Panhandle A&M College at the time who recognized these prehistoric artifacts, which were uncovered on farms and ranches, and were recovered and preserved.

More modern history of what is now Texas County in the Oklahoma Panhandle continues to reflect a colorful history. The area in No Man's Land had belonged to no state or nation for 70 years; before that, it had belonged to Spain, France, Mexico, and the Texas Republic at various times from the 1500s. In 1850, the state of Texas ceded to the US government land that had belonged to the Texas Republic, and its northern boundary as a slave state was set at the 36°30' parallel. When Kansas joined the Union, its southern boundary was established by the Missouri Compromise, but in 1854 it changed to the 37th parallel to make Kansas a free state, leaving a strip of land 34.5 miles wide and 167 miles long belonging to no state or nation.

When there was an attempt in 1886 to create a formal territory for that strip of land between 36°30' and the 37th parallel and the 100th and 103rd meridians, the area was called Beaver County, Cimarron Territory, with the capital in Beaver City. The only towns in existence at that time in the central area of the strip were Hardesty, Tyrone, and Optima. The few settlers were ranchers, such as the Hitches and the Millers, and those who settled the CCC and OX Ranches. There were ranchers from Texas who drove cattle through the area on the National Cattle Trail to load them on the trains at Optima and Shade's Well and ship them out of Liberal, Kansas, but they did not create permanent settlements.

When Cimarron Territory was tacked on to Oklahoma Territory in 1890, the entire area became Beaver County, or the Seventh County, again with Beaver City as the county seat. Texas County did not officially exist as a separate county until later when Beaver County was included in Oklahoma statehood in 1907. The area was then divided into three counties—Cimarron, Texas, and Beaver—with each having its own county seat.

Because the area belonged to other nations long before it was settled by those early ranchers and farmers, it has a unique background. That history is reflected in place names, settlements, and events that shaped the countryside. As there was no law and order for 70 years after the Anglos came, it harbored some who did not necessarily abide by any societal rules or legalities, making for a colorful past.

Other than the prehistoric settlements that might today be called towns, no towns existed in present-day Texas County until the late 1800s; even then, there were only three settlements that could be called towns: Hardesty, Optima, and Tyrone. Another tiny town called Buffalo existed for all of two years when its founders thought it would house the land office for new homesteaders. However, it was abandoned when the land office was established in Beaver City, the county seat of the Seventh County of Oklahoma Territory in 1890. These three original towns came about because of the ranching and cattle industries.

All the other towns in Texas County were built when the railroads came to the area in the early 1900s. Even Tyrone, which began in 1891 as a loading site for cattle to be shipped out of Liberal, Kansas, was moved in 1902 to its present site to be on the new Rock Island Railroad (CRI&P) as it began laying rails for a line across No Man's Land. Both Hardesty and Optima were moved from their original sites to be on the new railroad. The original town of Hardesty was settled four miles northeast of its present site in 1887. Optima began as a ranching community and a watering hole for cattlemen driving their herds to railcars in Liberal, Kansas. It was also moved closer to the railroad in 1902. The towns of Goodwell, Guymon, Hooker, Adams, Bakersburg (originally Eureka, then later Baker), Hough, and Eva served the railroad. Towns that existed for only a short time were Tracy, Muncy, and Cosmos.

These early attempts to bring in government and laws are unique and are a part of what is Texas County today. The pioneers who ranched, homesteaded, and helped found towns and villages and post offices and schools shaped the modern society the county citizens enjoy today. Those first lawyers, real estate brokers, railroad engineers, and doctors who helped found towns and establish businesses and practices in both the smaller and larger towns provided a support system for the financial success of the area. Those first oil and gas companies that risked capital to drill in the 1920s and later in the 1950s and bring pipelines added tremendously to the economy and growth of the area.

The history of Texas County provides insight into its prosperous growth into the 21st century, reflecting the brave and hearty pioneers who came to No Man's Land to ranch, then farm, and later build businesses and industry.

The entrepreneurs of the 20th century certainly brought jobs and opportunities to the people of Texas County. Without their leadership, feed yards, a packing plant, hog farms, and new businesses would not have been established. Oil, gas, and pipelines would not have brought major income to the county, and civic organizations, churches, and schools would not have existed. If not for the entrepreneurs, a four-year university would not have been a centerpiece of the county for a hundred years, nor would there be a research station from Oklahoma State University on the grounds of that four-year school.

Finally, when Oklahoma became a state, the strip was broken up into three counties, with Texas County being located between Beaver and Cimarron Counties, changing the area drastically. The coming of railroads at the beginning of the 20th century brought the most change, causing new towns to spring up, and the coming of homesteaders at about the same time created a whole new culture. It is from these humble beginnings that the area has grown and prospered and become a leader in gas production, hog farms, with a packing plant as well as prosperous farms and ranches. Excellent schools and a four-year university provide education for its citizens, as well as for the surrounding counties and states.

In reviewing the history of the area, the reader can see how modern entrepreneurs have continued that same leadership and "stick-to-it-ness" of the pioneers of early days, relying on their ideas and hard work. We thank them for carrying on that tradition.

One

Early History and Ranches

Until the coming of ranches into what is now Texas County, there were no permanent settlements other than the prehistoric ones that had been discovered in the 20th century. Modern-day Native Americans hunted buffalo and other game here, but because there was little water and few trees for shelter, this area was their hunting grounds. True, three families from Bernalillo, New Mexico Territory, had settled in what would become western Cimarron County as sheep ranchers to provide food for the Santa Fe Trail travelers, but none had settled east of there other than in eastern Beaver County. Some of the early ranchers came here because they had crossed the area as cowboys on cattle trails or because no one claimed the land, so it was essentially free to be claimed.

Some of these early ranches were discussed by Boss Neff in an interview with John McCarty, the editor and associate publisher for the Globe-News Publishing Company of Amarillo, Texas. According to Neff, when he first came to No Man's Land, there were already ranches in the area of what is now Texas County. The 101 Ranch ran its herd along the Texaquite, and the ZH Ranch was south of the Cimarron River into No Man's Land. These ranchers ran about 25,000 head of cattle.

Grimmer had the IB Ranch, situated west of Guymon on the Beaver River, and the OX Ranch was southeast of Guymon. E.C. Dudley's Ranch was above Grimmer's on the Beaver River, the Anchor D was on Hackberry Creek, and the Hardesty Brothers had the inverted-S Half Circle Ranch on Chiquita Creek. Not too much later, other ranches appeared on the range in Texas County. Boss Neff's Ranch had fenced in about 50 sections along the Beaver and Hackberry. By 1887, W.D. Miller and his sons C.R. (also known as Clay), Tom, and Ed had established a ranch as the others had done, with squatters' rights, later claiming homesteaders' rights when the area became part of Oklahoma Territory. Neighboring the Millers was the ranch founded by James K. Hitch with his father-in-law, Henry Westmoreland. Other ranches were the Myers, CCC, 101, Mayer, and many other smaller spreads.

Texas County does have a unique history. At various times, it has belonged to five different nations: Spain, France, Mexico, the United States, and the Republic of Texas. This does not count the Indian nations that have claimed it as their land. As no state or nation claimed it for more than 70 years, it was known as No Man's Land. Finally, this area became part of the Oklahoma Territory in 1890, then a county of the state of Oklahoma in 1907. (No Man's Land Historical Society.)

This is a copy of the seal that was made for what became the Cimarron Territory in 1886. It was hoped that No Man's Land would become a state of the United States, known as Cimarron. The first meeting to organize the territory was held at Beaver City in November 1886. Beaver City was the "capital" of the entire Oklahoma Panhandle at that time. Dr. O.G. Chase was elected to Congress and went to Washington, DC, to secure recognition and admission of Cimarron Territory to the United States. All attempts to become a state failed. (NMLHS.)

This picture shows the book containing the minutes of efforts trying to establish a state known as Cimarron. At a meeting, Cimarron Territory was divided into three districts and then enlarged to five counties. From east to west were Benton, Beaver, Hardesty, Optima, and Mineral. The only efforts to organize the counties were made in Benton and Beaver. Beaver City was chosen as the county seat of Beaver County and the capital of Cimarron Territory. Dr. O.G. Chase, as well as J.E. Dale, had gone to Congress to establish the new state of Cimarron, but both failed. This book can be seen at the No Man's Land Museum in Goodwell. (NMLHS.)

The open range of No Man's Land looked like this before man and his plow turned it over. Grasses were the main reason the buffalo (and later, the cattlemen) were attracted to these high plains. Note the antelope in the background. While the wild buffalo are gone, antelope can still be seen in Texas County. (Dr. Harold Kachel.)

The Hitch Ranch is one of the oldest and largest ranches in the Panhandle. It was established by James K. Hitch with his father-in-law, Henry Westmoreland. Their brand, the OX, was seen on cattle in three states. (Hitch family archives.)

Henry C. Hitch assumed direction of the ranch in 1921, expanding the operation and building a feedlot on the ranch in 1953. (*The Encyclopedia of Oklahoma History and Culture.*)

Henry Hitch Jr., better known as "Ladd," opened three high-capacity commercial feedlots by the mid-1970s. Hitch Enterprises eventually grew to include the ranch, 10,000 acres of farmland, the three feedlots, a cattle-buying company, a company that financed feed cattle operations, a commercial cowherd, and pig production facilities. (EncyOHC and Hitch family archives.)

The children of Henry C. and Christine Hitch are pictured here in the back row, from left to right, Jane Hitch Gray, Ladd Hitch, and Marjorie Hitch Price. (Hitch family archives.)

Pictured here are three generations of Hitches at the H.C. Hitch Jr. home. From left to right are (first row) Karick Asa Price, Paul Hitch, Jane Hitch, Jim Hitch in front of Christine Gray, and Brad Gray; (second row) Henry Hitch, Christine Hitch, Lala Moores Hitch, Ladd Hitch, Joyce Hitch Gray, John Bradford Gray, Marjorie Hitch Price, and W.K. Price Jr. (Hitch family archives.)

The OX was the brand used by the Hitch Ranch. Pictured in front of the house is the Hightower family. (NMLHS.)

Green Ranch Headquarters house, built in 1896, was located east of Hardesty and near the Palo Creek in eastern Texas County. This two-story mansion for its time, standing on the prairie, was quite a sight to come upon in these plains. Another unique thing about the house is that it is constructed of rock from northeast of Hardesty. (Dr. Harold Kachel.)

The rock house headquarters of the CCC Ranch, pictured here, later became part of the Freeman Ranch. (NMLHS.)

Pictured here is the remodeled house on the CCC Ranch, which was owned by the Coons family and later bought by the Freemans. Today, it is more commonly known as the Freeman Ranch. (Freeman family archives.)

The Anchor D Ranch was established in 1878 on the Beaver River. At one time, owners Ezra Dudley and his son John owned land from Kansas to Texas across what would one day become Texas County and pastured 30,000 head of cattle on 960,000 acres. Ancient writing and initials can be found on a rock, along with the Anchor D brand, north of the present town of Goodwell near a former Indian camp. Recently, it has been owned by the Stoneciphers and by the Freemans. In this picture, Jack Freeman watches his cattle as he feeds them. (EncyOHC and Freeman Ranch archives.)

This image of branding cattle on the Miller Ranch shows W.D. Miller, the father of C.R.; Tom; and Ed Miller. C.R. and Tom sit on the ground. The Millers had come to nearby Liberal, Kansas, to work on laying the new railroad, then began their ranch in 1889 east and south of what would much later become Guymon. (Charles Dean Miller.)

The Charlie Hitch Ranch roundup in the 1930s featured eight-year-old Gene R. Miller, in the foreground with the cap on. Charlie had invited his neighbors in for the day of fun. Note the wide-open spaces. (Charles Dean Miller.)

Charlie Hitch is on one of his favorite horses. The alertness of the horse is a result of a cowboy spending weeks breaking and training the animal to ride. This photograph was taken in 1934. (Charles Dean Miller.)

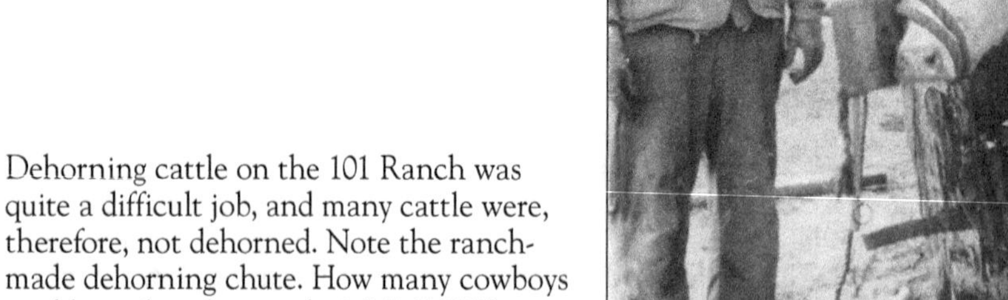

Dehorning cattle on the 101 Ranch was quite a difficult job, and many cattle were, therefore, not dehorned. Note the ranch-made dehorning chute. How many cowboys could use this chute today? (NMLHS.)

This wedding picture of C.R. and Anna Miller of the old Miller Ranch was taken in August of 1898. C.R. was the son of W.D. Miller, who started the Miller Ranch ten miles east and four miles south of the present-day Guymon in 1889. (Charles Dean Miller.)

By 1910, C.R. Miller was solidly established on the ranch. Shown here are C.R. and his wife, Anna, with their children Clay, Ada, and Alta. (Charles Dean Miller.)

Pictured here is C.R. Miller of the C.R. Miller Ranch (Charles Dean Miller.)

In 1939, the Earl and Rosa (Henning) Dixon family lived on land they homesteaded northwest of Guymon. Pictured from left to right are (first row) Ernest, Earl, Bonnie, Rosa, and Gerald; (second row) Kay, Oral, Earlene, and John. Five of these children remained in the Guymon area and worked in business and farming. Although they never referred to their farming interests northwest of Guymon as a ranch, it became extensive in both Texas and Cimarron Counties. (Gerald Dixon.)

Pictured here is a horse-drawn cook shack or wagon used on the Dixon farm around 1912 through the 1920s. The cook shack moved with the workmen as they performed their duties of the day. These duties would include branding, working cattle, or going on a cattle drive. It could be a threshing crew in harvest time who needed to be fed. (Gerald Dixon.)

Boss Sebastian Neff was born in Ohio on March 5, 1866, and died on March 15, 1947. In his early years, he decided to go west and ended up in the Panhandles of Texas and Oklahoma. He worked on several of the large ranches in a variety of jobs. He also made a few tries at cattle drives to other ranges and cattle markets. Eventually, Boss started his own ranch and ended up in the Beaver River and Coldwater Creek area. With his interest in history, he supported and was president of the No Man's Land Historical Society of Goodwell, Oklahoma, for a number of years. (Boss Ira "Bud" Neff.)

Ira J. Neff, the older brother of Boss Neff, ranched on the Cimarron River. By 1887, he had settled on the south end of Palo Duro Creek. Ira was fond of a good dog and usually had one around. Ira's ranch was some three miles from the CCC Ranch. (Boss Ira "Bud" Neff.)

Boss Ira "Bud" Neff, whose father was Ira S. "Boss" Neff, is a grandson of Boss Sebastian Neff. He grew up on and lived on the Neff Ranch for a time and now lives in Garden City, Kansas. (Boss Ira "Bud" Neff.)

Members of the Ranchers' Association, Texas County included Curt Ricrert, Charlie Hitch, C.R. Miller, Jim Hedon, Boss Neff, Con Jackson, Jim England, (Bertha?) Loofbourrow, Bill Ewing, Lee Larrabee, and Bill George. (Charles Dean Miller.)

The cowboys and ranch owners were very proud of their horses. When barbed wire came into this area and was used to hold animals in an enclosed paddock, they became suspicious of the barbs cutting the horses. Because of this, the wire shown in the picture was their choice. This high-tensile spiral non-sag wire was patented by J.L. Riter on October 10, 1893. (Dr. Harold Kachel.)

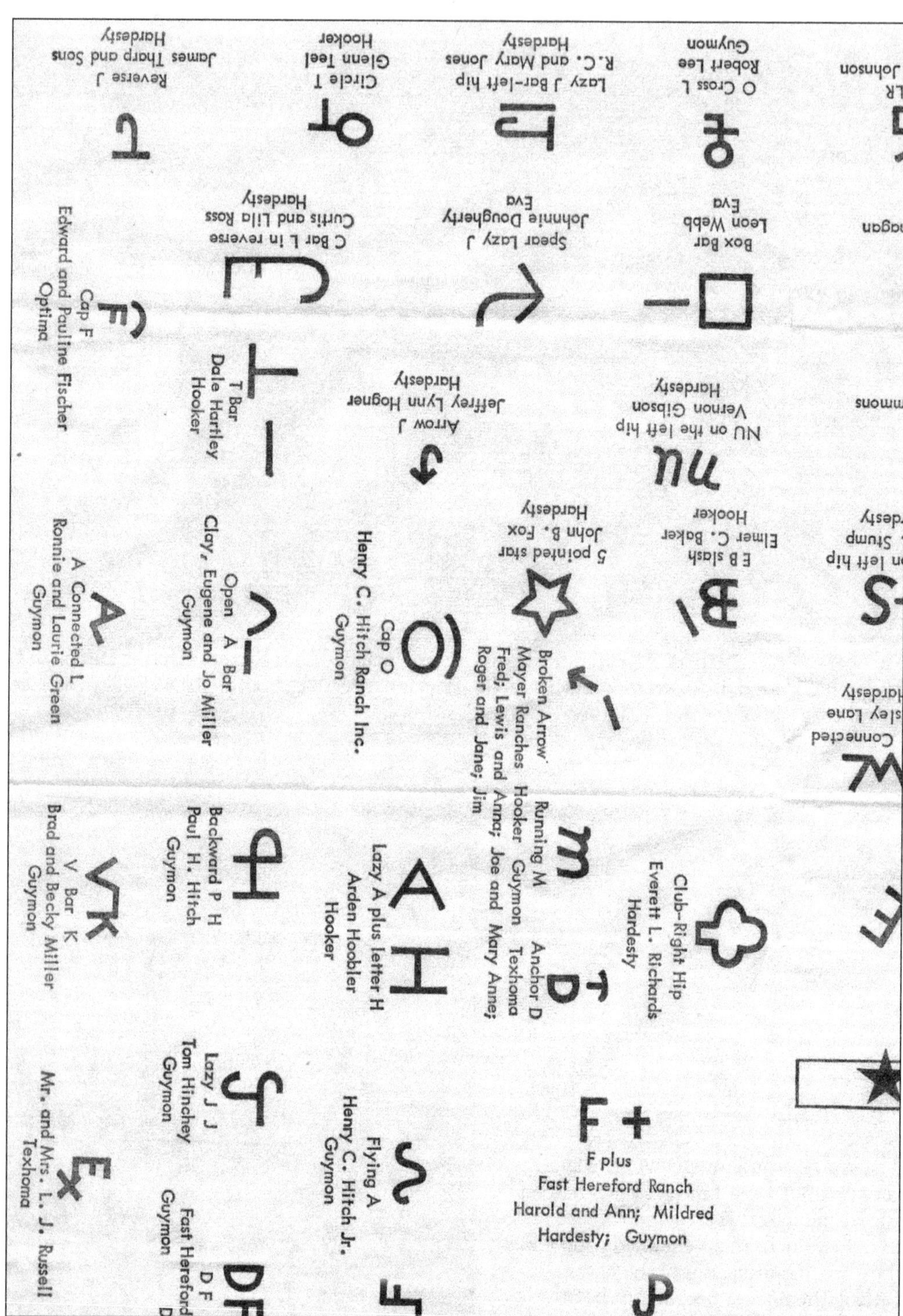

Some of the cattle brands of Texas County are featured here. Names of brands were often used to identify the ranch itself. (Dr. Harold Kachel.)

Two

Prehistory and Anthropology

Texas County has several archaeology and anthropology sites within its boundaries. The archaeological sites in Texas County extend from 400 years ago to perhaps 20,000 years ago or more. The Oklahoma of the past had a milder climate, with cooler summers and warmer winters, which encouraged the growth of better grasslands in modern-day Western Oklahoma. This, in turn, produced a great number of larger animals such as the bison.

In time, this caused the Indians to move into the area and establish such sites as the Lloyd Tucker kill site, Stamper Optima site, the Two Sisters site, and the McGrath, Johnson-Cline, and Charles Rhoton sites, as well as others. Between 13,000 and 5,000 years ago, the climate again gradually warmed, producing a change in the vegetation cover, and the animals and people had to adapt or become extinct. It is believed that this period saw the mammoth become extinct in the area.

All the images within this chapter are from the archives of Dr. Harold Kachel.

The Stamper archeological site, situated northeast of Guymon, is also called the Optima site. This camp was excavated by the faculty and students of the University of Oklahoma. The Stamper camp was one of the first excavated in the Oklahoma Panhandle. This site is dated to the early 1400s and was dug in the 1930s.

This is all that was still standing of one of the Two Sisters houses built northeast of Guymon by Clarence McGrath, father of sisters Edna and Emanuella McGrath of Boston, when the Two Sisters archeological site was excavated.

The Two Sisters site was excavated by members of the University of Oklahoma archeological department in the 1960s. These houses, occupied during the 1400s, are believed to be part of the Antelope Creek phase of Indian culture.

The remains of an Indian camp show scattered campfire rocks. This site is east of the Yarbrough School in what was once a wheat field. This image exhibits the extreme wind erosion of the 1950s dry period in Texas County. The only plants holding on are the soap weeds, also known as yucca plants.

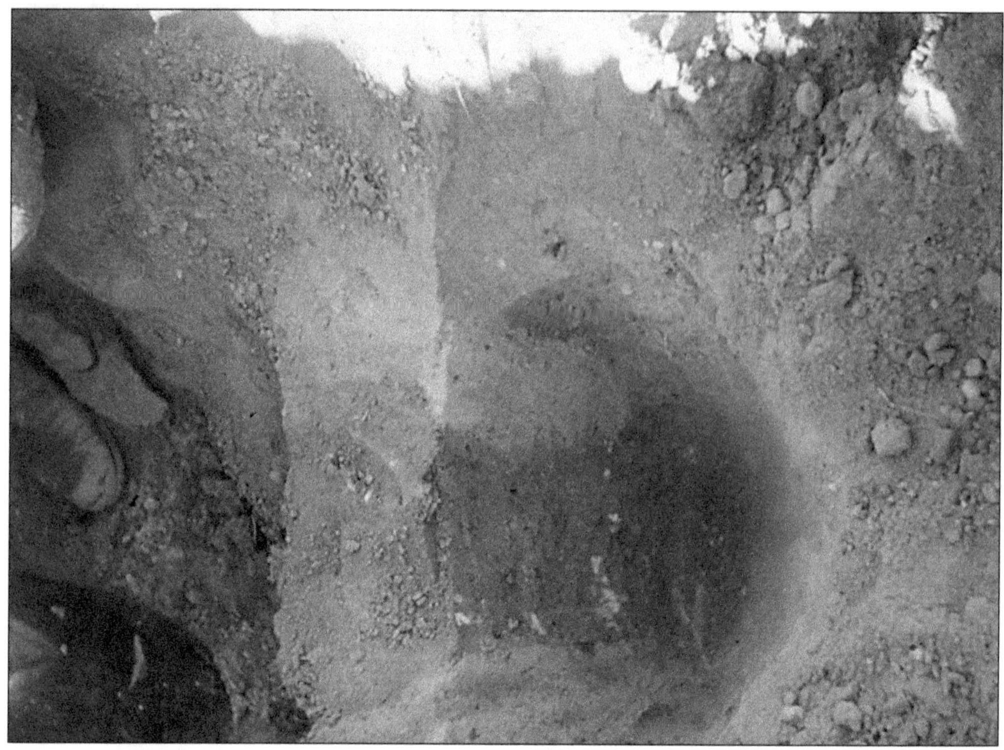

This is a picture of a very rare, lined, hardened-clay cooking pot buried in the ground. This cooking pot was discovered and dug out by pot hunters at a camp site east of Guymon. Very few examples of this type of pot have been found. This one was filled with trash when it was excavated.

An unexcavated Indian campsite north of Texhoma sits along the Beaver River. Notice that someone has dug in the center of this spot. The rocks seen were once the foundation stones of a house, forming the beginning of the outer walls, normally some two feet below the level-ground surface. This site contains evidence of several other houses.

This photograph shows where an Indian campfire had once been. This wheat field was blown down to the hardpan during the 1950s near Eva, Oklahoma. The plain marks and few camp rocks around the burnt area where the fire had been are still evident. There were several other similar areas in this field.

Joan Kachel stands across the road from the Yarbrough School near an Indian campsite. At the time this image was captured, she was the Yarbrough School's secretary during the 1950s when this field blew out and left these eroded foundations. The Indian site she stands near is the Charles Rhoton archaeology site, where several artifacts were found, along with the remains of what appeared to be a home.

These rocks have all once been in circles of different sizes. Located north of Goodwell along the Beaver River and part of the Anchor D Ranch, these stones are usually part of what are called tepee rings; however, the author believes they are rather associated with garden plots. Rocks on the ground hold and conserve water; thus, the seeds planted beside them have a better chance to survive. These rings of different sizes are also found on the high plains.

If this Indian petroglyph is authentic, it is the only one known to exist in Texas County. This petroglyph does seem to be older than the other drawings and designs found in this locale. While someone had chalked over this petroglyph to make it show up better, this procedure destroys the ability to tell its age. This petroglyph was also found near the tepee rings north of Goodwell along the Beaver River. The stick drawing of the people is very unusual for the Indian methods of depicting people. It should probably be classified as a pictograph.

This Indian fire pit was blown out in the 1950s near Goff Creek in Texas County. The stones are still rather large and not broken up yet. Perhaps it was not used many times before it was abandoned. Notice more stones scattered in the background. It is believed that many of these fire pits found in the area date back to the 1400s, the time when there were permanent houses in the area, such as at the Stamper site.

Those who hunt for Indian artifacts as a hobby can understand the feeling of walking across a field that has been blown out and seeing this sight. One wonders how many hundreds of years that point has laid there.

These archeological sites became known as belonging to the Panhandle aspect of the Antelope Creek of the Texas Panhandle Pueblo culture. Now, the Texas County sites are usually referred to as the Washita Focus and the Optima Focus. Archeologists cannot say which tribes came to this area in later years, but they believe they were from the Caddoan groups. It was in the 1600s, before tribes such as the Comanche, Apache, and the Kiowa started moving into the Panhandle area.

Pictured here are the eggs of the Killdeer bird, which typically lay their eggs in rocky, wide-open areas.

Three

Early Farming

By the time the lands in Texas County really opened up for farming, the farmers had learned some lessons from the failures of cooperatives in the Grange period, a time in which groups were formed to try to get better prices for their products. Also, the previous marketing and purchasing associations that had been formed had given up their practice and let the farmers practice better business ideas on their own. Improved machinery helped them to produce more, and they invented new equipment. Some improvements were the gasoline engine, the seed drill, new cultivators, mowing machines, binders, and later, self-propelled equipment.

In Texas County, the land and moisture supply was suited for wheat, broomcorn, some corn, and other small grains such as Kafir corn and maize. Turkey Red wheat was one of the first to be planted, and had been brought to this area by European immigrants. Black Hull was also an early variety of wheat planted in Texas County. These two were crossed together to form a new variety called Wichita, which became a favorite for many farmers. By 1929, Texas County was producing more winter wheat than any other county in the nation. The tractors, combines, drills, one-way plows, and other improved farming machines paved the way for large farms and changed all phases of the older farming culture. Perhaps these changes have also contributed to the unseen coming of the Dust Bowl.

Those who still ranched had two things they worried about the most: the prairie fires and the loco weed. The loco weed usually came up first in the spring. It was very green and poisonous and made the cattle go crazy, not eating their food, running through fences, and foaming at the mouth. Of course, the farmers' use of barbed wire and plowing up of virgin pasture was also a concern.

Many farmers preferred to use mules in their operations, as they believed the animals could work longer and harder and were easier to take care of than a horse. The mule is a cross between a mare horse and a jackass or donkey. In this picture, three mules and one horse work together. (NMLHS.)

Perhaps these passengers are on their way to work or church; however, the umbrella still looks out of place on this type of wagon. Here, there are pairs of horses and mules pulling the wagons. This was the main mode of transportation at this time, although the road they are on appears well defined. (NMLHS.)

A small grain header is at work in a wheat field. Hauling the cut wheat to be stacked in large piles are the horse-drawn barges. A freight wagon with the backside much higher than the front is used to help hold in the loose grain stacks. One man is on top of the stack as the wheat barge is being loaded onto the pile. This stack will remain here until the threshing crew shows up. (NMLHS.)

A.G. Briles harvests hay in this 1918 photograph, which was taken near the future town of Adams. The town was established in 1930 with the coming of the railroad. (NMLHS.)

No one seems to know for sure what this implement was used for, but it looks as though it could have been an early type of rod weeder or the forerunner of the Graham-Hoeme plow. At any rate, it is being pulled by a caterpillar-type tractor, indicating heavy weight. Standing beside the tractor are the Jamison brothers. (Clyde Jamison.)

This machine is called a feed binder. Instead of cutting the crop and leaving it loose, it went one step further and tied it into a bundle, saving the farmer much time and effort by making it easier to move it from one place to another. The bundles were then placed together in shocks, which each usually contained from 20 to 30 bundles. They were then moved to the threshing machine. The Deering Company, part of the International Harvester Company, later the McCormick Deering Company or the IHC Company, was probably the first to produce the binder. (NMLHS.)

The Ducket brothers lived with their large crop of maize somewhat south of Baker, Oklahoma, in 1914. These piles are only the heads of the maize plant and were cut off by hand, then thrown into a header barge to be hauled to these stacks. They then were threshed. (Joe Lawder.)

At times, a large caravan traveling together took the grain from a threshing crew to the nearest elevator or railroad to be sold. Mules and horses were used to pull the loaded wagons. (NMLHS.)

Covered-wagon mule teams were used to haul the maize crop to elevators. (NMLHS.)

As tractors were invented, threshing became easier and faster. (NMLHS.)

The development of the gasoline tractor and machines that threshed the grain as it was harvested increased how fast the harvest could be cut and grain stored in the bin. Pictured below are A.J. William and crew. (Both, NMLHS.)

The invention of the modern combine and gasoline-powered trucks for harvesting small grains once again changed the picture of farming. It was another leap in the number of acres that could be planted or harvested in one day, and once again farms grew in size and productivity. Modern machinery also allowed more virgin pasture to be plowed up, perhaps a harbinger of the Dust Bowl to come. (NMLHS.)

Four

Dirty Thirties and Fifties Years

Many people have wondered what caused the Dust Bowl in the Oklahoma Panhandle and adjoining states beginning in the 1930s. Of course, the lack of rain was a contributing factor, but the area had seen long dry periods before. Perhaps one of the causes of the blowing dust was the people themselves, especially those who called themselves farmers.

Texas County's population grew greatly during the 1910s and 1920s. The land had been settled in quarter sections by homesteaders who came from areas such as Missouri, Iowa, and Illinois where moisture was usually plentiful, and most of the large ranches were gone. The farmers now had tractors and the one-way plow, and they could plow hundreds of acres of native grasses per day. And plow they did. The rain came, and the prices for crops were high for the times; wheat, maize, and broomcorn were cash crops and grew well on the flat plains. Then no rain or other moisture fell for 10 years. No cover crops or grasses were left. The wind had its say blowing the topsoil away.

The 1930s brought on some new ideas about the way to farm because of the dry weather. Contour farming and two new tools for working the soil, the chisel plow and the large flat-bladed plow, were tested. The Graham-Hoeme plow was first used near Hooker, Oklahoma, and the Bultimans farm in Texas County was one of the first to use the sweep plow. These two units left much of the foliage on top of the ground, while the one-way plow had turned it under the ground. Because of this, during a 1950s drought, the area saw fewer dirt storms and blowing dust. Strip farming methods were also used. Some government programs helped with farmers being able to use new methods and leave fewer acres bare. These were the Soil Bank programs, the building of farm ponds, and land terracing.

When the tractor and the one-way plow became the favorite tools of the trade, the land could be worked on rapidly. The one-way turned the soil and residue under the ground and left very little on top. This method of working the ground did not help hold the soil in place or reduce the moisture evaporation. This contributed to the dirt storms of the 1930s. (NMLHS.)

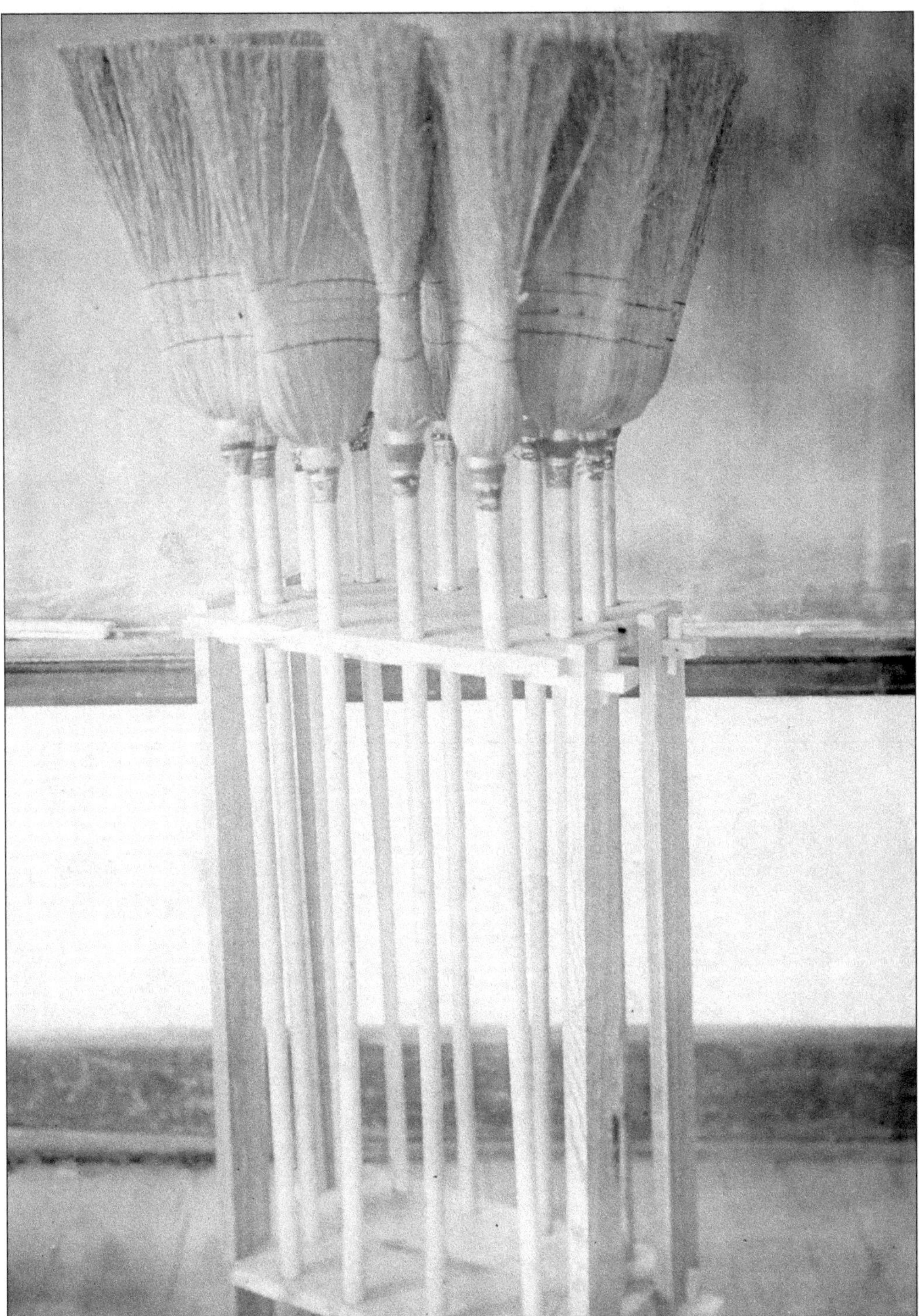

One of the cash crops for the farmers in Texas County in the early part of the 20th century was broomcorn, which produced the main ingredient in the making of brooms. Broomcorn first appeared in 1889 in No Man's Land, which would later become the Panhandle of Oklahoma. (Dr. Harold Kachel.)

The experiment station pictured here on the farm campus of the Pan-Handle Agricultural Institute (PAI) outside Goodwell, later to become Panhandle A&M College, tried many different crops in the area and, later, different types of farming methods. (NMLHS.)

The Dirty Thirties came to Texas County, almost the very heart of the Dust Bowl region. This picture was taken by the Wilson Studio of Texhoma, Oklahoma, on April 14, 1935, a date commonly known as Black Sunday. This was one of the most violent storms in the region during this era. (NMLHS.)

This picture of a dust storm in Guymon, Oklahoma, was taken in 1933. It exhibits the intensity of the blowing dirt and why these storms spread fear among many of the people. (Hurlimann family.)

This image shows how the dust storms rolled in. They seemed to be tumbling over and over as they came across the plains. Usually, a lack of moving air or almost no wind preceded the dust storm. This photograph was taken in 1937. (NMLHS.)

This abandoned farm shows the results of farming practices in Texas County by the end of the Dirty Thirties. These terrible conditions covered parts of five states and lasted almost nine years. Many farmers left, and most of the abandoned farmsteads have been leveled. Only a few memories remain among those people who lived through this period. (NMLHS.)

As the 1930s were coming to a close, the US Department of Agriculture got involved by helping the experiment stations with ideas and new methods of farming. This picture, taken at the Panhandle Agriculture and Mechanical College (PAMC) experiment station, shows one new method of farming known as contour farming. The rows of crops were all planted on the same level or grade of ground to help hold the water where it fell. This method probably helped produce strip farming and contour farming to control soil erosion. (NMLHS.)

William E. "Uncle Bill" Baker was an Oklahoma state extension agent, mainly for Cimarron County, but he traveled and worked a large area that included the Goodwell unit. He was also associated with the No Man's Land Historical Society and the museum for many years. He donated a large Indian collection to the No Man's Land Museum. Baker was never without his wide-brimmed hat and his handlebar mustache. (NMLHS.)

The farm at Panhandle Agriculture and Mechanical College Farm grew many plants and crops to teach students improved farming methods. This farm also produced almost all of the vegetables, milk, and meat used in the college cafeteria. (NMLHS.)

The 1940s brought moisture and good crops to most of Texas County, and the farmers and ranchers were encouraged that they would not see another dry period as they had in the 1930s. However, the 1950s changed that, and drought again returned. If there were some rains that came at the right time, the yucca plants would be out in full bloom. These yucca plants (or soap weeds) were found in what was a wheat field in the 1930s that never recovered. This field along Goff Creek still has a lot of wind erosion today. (Dr. Harold Kachel.)

Extensive erosion of a field near Goff Creek by wind and water action is seen here. About the only things living are some yucca plants. Indian camp rocks are also visible. (Dr. Harold Kachel.)

Pictured here is a rabbit drive held in the Goff Creek Valley area in the 1950s. The rabbits did well in this dry spell and became overpopulated. They had eaten almost all of the vegetation in the pasture, which had begun to blow away by then. Very little, if any, cover material was left where the rabbits had become so abundant. (Dr. Harold Kachel.)

An abandoned farmstead in the 1950s shows drifts of dirt that occurred during this period. Maybe not as much dirt moved as in the 1930s, but it was just as dry (or drier). (Dr. Harold Kachel.)

By the 1980s, several new practical farming methods were being used. One was the Graham-Hoeme plow, shown here. The advantage of this type of tool is that it left most of the cover crop on top of the ground. Graham and Hoeme of Hooker, Oklahoma, invented and used this type of implement first. The plow in the picture, a Model A, serial no. 449, was used by Sam W. Kachel. In the background is the one-way plow the Graham-Hoeme plow replaced. (Dr. Harold Kachel.)

The blade plow, or sweeper plow, was being completed about the same time as the Graham-Hoeme plow. It took longer to perfect the blades for the plow before the farmer started using it. Large flat blades run under the soil, lift up, and then drop it back where it was. Almost all the vegetation is left on top of the ground to help cut down on wind erosion and water evaporation. The driver of this tractor, Lea Kachel Morgan, works the terraced field with this sweep plow. The terraces are another method to control erosion. (Dr. Harold Kachel.)

New methods of planting and soil management led to less soil erosion, so that when droughts came, the damage was not as serious as it was in the 1930s. (Clyde Jamison.)

In 1933, Riffe Elevator at Texhoma struggled to fill its silos, unlike in the 1920s, when the great plow-up led to the Dust Bowl. (Hurlimann family.)

Springtime in Texas County can be very colorful. If the rains come at the right time, the prairie will sprout many types of wild flowers. Some of these plants may not have bloomed in years, but if the conditions are just right, they will, from wild sweet peas to fields of yellow to the state wild flower: the Indian blanket (Gaillardia). Do not confuse the state wild flower with the state flower: the mistletoe. (Dr. Harold Kachel.)

Five

Early Towns

The first towns in Texas County grew out of the need for post offices and general stores to supply the needs of the few ranchers. It was not until the homesteaders, sometimes called "punkin' rollers" by the ranchers, and the coming of the railroads to haul the crops produced by these new settlers that towns were created and thrived. The three early towns that grew out of ranching and cattle trails moved to the new rail sites: Hardesty, Optima, and Tyrone. Optima began as a ranching and cattle trail community in 1885. It was moved to its present location in 1901 to be on the new railroad. By 1918, there was the First State Bank and four general stores. In 1920, it had a high school district. W.H. Miller was the first postmaster in Optima in 1886. New towns were created about every 10 miles to provide water and other necessities at railroad switches as the CRI&P and, later, the Beaver, Meade and Englewood Railroad (BM&E) crossed what would become Texas County. Of these 15 towns, only nine survived and most of those are villages today. Of the early settlements, some only survived a year or so, some lasted until the railroads removed tracks in their area, and some died in the Dust Bowl. The major towns today are Guymon, Hooker, Texhoma, and Goodwell, with Tyrone, Optima, Hardesty, Adams, and Baker still in existence with a few stores, and a school in some cases. Those that survived are an example of the hearty folk who braved the elements to develop farms, towns, and schools in No Man's Land.

One of the earliest towns in Texas County was Tyrone, which was promoted by railroad officials in the summer of 1888 when the Rock Island Railroad began laying rails for a spur into No Man's Land. (NMLHS.)

This is a street scene in early Tyrone. By 1891, Charlie Hitch reported that the town consisted of saloons, gamblers, and girls. The original Tyrone was located close to Shade's Well, just two miles south, where a windmill supplied water for cattle waiting to be loaded onto railcars and shipped out of nearby Liberal, Kansas. (JoDean James.)

The First National Bank in Tyrone was one of the earliest banks in the area. (Lidia Hook Gray.)

Guy and Fred Speakman were some of the first customers of the First National Bank of Tyrone. (Lidia Hook Gray.)

This early dry-cleaning business in Tyrone was one of the first businesses in the new town. (J.M. Hughes and JoDean James.)

In this 1907 Tyrone street scene, the bank, drugstore, and railroad station are in the background. (Lidia Hook Gray.)

Pleasant Ridge was built in 1910 in the northwest quarter of section 2, township 1, range 19. Sunday school and literary events were also held in the building. (JoDean James.)

This American Legion World War I monument was dedicated May 11, 1922, in Tyrone. (Lidia Hook Gray.)

Pictured here is Optima School after it was built to house grades 1–12 in 1919. Although the original town of Optima was established in 1886, it was not until the town was moved that a formal school district was established. The Optima School was remodeled in 2007 and is now an elementary district. (Supt. Rex Hale, Optima School.)

Pictured here is the Range Community Church in Hardesty. The original townsite of Hardesty, situated four miles northeast of the present site, had a store, a saloon, a wagon yard, and several sod houses. The town was moved when the CRI&P Railroad bypassed the original site. It was moved six and half miles away from the new railroad switch. The nearby community of Range was a vital part of Hardesty when it moved. (*Hardesty History*.)

The Range School was one of the 19 elementary schools that consolidated with Hardesty when the old town of Hardesty was moved. The Range School was housed in Woodman Hall, then in a dugout, and finally, in a new building where the school was initially called Hominy before it changed its name to Range. (*Hardesty History*.)

In this photograph, mail carrier J.O. Tansy takes mail from Range to Hardesty. He and other carriers often carried mail on to Guymon and returned on the route. (*Hardesty History*.)

Pictured in 1913, the Hardesty Methodist Church met in this rock church for nearly 60 years. (*Hardesty History*.)

The Methodist church, situated on Highway 3, was built in Hardesty in 1974 and still serves the community today. (*Hardesty History*.)

Pictured here are the students and staff of Hardesty Elementary School with teachers relegated to squatting in the first row. (NMLHS.)

The Hardesty High School basketball team is pictured here in 1923. From left to right are (first row) Lloyd Ricker, Roy Lilleton, Lynn Ricker, and Marlin Hale; (second row) Sen. Leon Fields (teacher), Joe Morris, Paul Hale, and Everest Allen (*Hardesty History*.)

This is an early Guymon street scene. Guymon had originally been known as Sanford when it was located on the new CRI&P Railroad at Sanford switch in 1902. Later, in 1904, the name was changed in honor of E.T. Guymon, land developer and promoter of the townsite company. (NMLHS.)

In 1902, a free-for-all race in the new town of Sanford was held before the name of the town was changed to Guymon. (NMLHS.)

Pictured here is the Beaver County Bank located in Guymon, Oklahoma Territory. At that time, Beaver County included the entire Panhandle area. (NMLHS.)

When Oklahoma became a state, the Panhandle was divided into three counties instead of the original one, Beaver (or the Seventh County, as it had been known in Oklahoma Territory times). Guymon won the title of county seat of the middle county, Texas, in 1907. This picture was taken in the bustling new town in 1909. (Hurlimann.)

Stanley Tyler had established the V-Z Bar Ranch in Hansford County, Texas, before moving to Guymon in 1907, where he was a retail merchant. He had been the son of a wealthy banking family in Massachusetts and attended Harvard University. (Tyler and Geraldine Latham.)

Louis E. Latham was born in Meridian, Mississippi, in 1879 and came to Guymon in 1904 to run a dry goods store. He and the Denny brothers built the first brick building in Guymon on the west side of Main Street. He later established Latham's Dry Goods Store at the corner of Fourth and Main Streets. He married Mary Angeline, daughter of Stanley C. Tyler, in 1908. (Tyler and Geraldine Latham.)

The children of Louis and Mary Latham were Tyler Latham and Mary Lou Latham Peppers. (Tyler and Geraldine Latham.)

Pictured here are Tyler Latham, wife Geraldine, and their children Beth and Louis, who are descendants of both pioneer families: the Tylers and the Lathams. (Tyler and Geraldine Latham.)

In this image, loyal customers stand in front of the Denny Bros. & Latham Dry Goods Store in Guymon. (NMLHS.)

This 1928 photograph of Main Street in Guymon shows the courthouse under construction. (NMLHS.)

L. Ennis came to No Man's Land from Arkansas in 1905 and established a real estate office in Guymon. He was active in real estate, buying land in Cimarron and Texas Counties, as well as mineral rights. He was very successful and bought a 1910 Buick to take his customers in to view properties. He retired from active business in 1941 but kept his office in the First National Bank building until his death in 1965. (Gerald Dixon.)

Pictured are the five surviving children of Earl and Rosa Dixon, from left to right, Bonnie, Earlene, Oral, Gerald, and Ernest. The first four have remained in the Guymon area as productive community citizens. Gerald credits L. Ennis with being his mentor and "teacher" all of his adult years after Dixon returned to Guymon from his jockey life. (Gerald Dixon.)

Crowds gather for Guymon Pioneer Days in 1933. This was an important day in hard times when not much recreation could be afforded. (NMLHS.)

The crowds return for Pioneer Days in 1934, even though the Dust Bowl and Depression were hitting the area hard. (NMLHS.)

These three citizens head off to Guymon Pioneer Days in 1934 for a grand time. (NMLHS.)

The Guymon Teachers' Institute was held in 1909 as training for public school teachers, who, at that time, did not have to have more than an eighth-grade diploma to teach students. Teachers from all three counties in the Panhandle attended. (NMLHS.)

The new Guymon Public School is pictured here upon completion. Note that the yard is so new, it has not been cleaned up yet. (NMLHS.)

The Guymon High School football team is in uniform here in 1909. Note the lack of protective gear that students wear today. (NMLHS.)

Here is the Methodist Episcopal church in Guymon as it looked in 1910 when Guymon was just beginning to grow. (Victory Memorial Methodist Church.)

This is the new Methodist Episcopal church in Guymon in 1913, built when the congregation had outgrown its former building. (VMMC.)

The Goodwell Implement Company was owned by W.W. Grooms, Ross Oldaker, and Jim Prevett in 1929. Goodwell officially became a town with the coming of the CRI&P Railroad in 1903, although the post office was not established until late in 1903. The railroad had a well dug that produced good water for its use, hence the town's name. (NMLHS.)

The Goodwell Hotel on Main Street in the center of the new town was important to those folk doing business with the Panhandle A&M College, located just a few blocks away. (NMLHS.)

Pictured here is the Goodwell High School in the 1940s. This building replaced the original school before the present-day building was erected. (NMLHS.)

The Goodwell Community Building and Fire Department were built to protect not only the town and school but also the nearby college. (NMLHS.)

The acquisition of Pan-Handle Agricultural Institute in Goodwell brought a blessing for the town as well as for area students. What became a high school for agriculture and home economics training later became a four-year college, then a state university. The group in this picture lays the cornerstone for the A&M College it would eventually become. (NMLHS.)

"Daddy" Black, the first president of Pan-Handle Agricultural Institute, is pictured here with his wife. The nickname was affectionately given to him by the students. (NMLHS.)

Students at PAI attend a class in 1913. Note the number of women in relation to men. (NMLHS.)

One of the integral parts of an education at PAI, and later, at PAMC, would be students' experience at the college farm. The farm, seen in this early photograph, also provided food for the student cafeteria. NMLHS.)

This view of Goodwell in 1913 shows one of the first buildings in town and the campus that would become Oklahoma Panhandle State University. (NMLHS.)

In nine years, the campus of the Pan-Handle Agricultural Institute grew, as did the town, with more new buildings added. Pictured on the right is Hesper Hall, to the left is Earle Hall, and in the center is the cafeteria. When the Rock Island Railroad first came through, it bypassed the original site of Texhoma that had served as a post office for the CCC Ranch and other settlers. The new site was established in 1901. By 1908, the town had a population of about 1,000. The depot was originally set in Oklahoma. In 1907, the Texas Railroad Commission ordered a depot be built on the Texas side to avoid fees from shipping cattle and goods from Oklahoma. The depot was then rebuilt to straddle the state lines and customers could ship from both states without the extra fees! (NMLHS.)

This sign for Texhoma advertises that the town sits across the state line and proclaims some of the benefits it has to offer. (Texhoma Museum.)

In the 1920s, things looked very prosperous for Texhoma, giving residents a reason to celebrate. Note the speed limit and driving directions for the Model Ts and other cars in town. (*Ten Decades of Texhoma 1901–2001.*)

Texhoma High School is the home of the Red Devils. (Texhoma Museum.)

Pictured here is one of the original elevators at Hooker, founded in 1904 when the CRI&P built tracks from Liberal, Kansas, to Texhoma. (Joe Lawder.)

Modern-day Hooker sits on both a major railroad and on National Highways 54 and 64. It was named in honor of the OX Ranch foreman John "Hooker" Threlkeld, a seasoned roper of cattle. By 1907, the town had grown to 448 folks. (Dr. Harold Kachel.)

Customers in Baker stand in front of the Bob Sellers Store, one of the first businesses in town. The town was originally named Bakersburg in 1939 when the BM&E Railroad stretched from Beaver County to Hooker. The original town, named Eureka, moved to the new site. However, the town kept the name Eureka for its school. (Joe Lawder.)

A building from the original town of Eureka, possibly the schoolhouse, was one of those moved from the original town site to the newly named Bakersburg. (Joe Lawder.)

Drilling the city well for the new town of Bakersburg was critical to provide water, not only for the townsfolk but also for the steam engine trains. (Joe Lawder.)

Bakersburg's Main Street in 1939 was a central part of providing rail service west to Hooker, as well as possibly south to Amarillo if new lines were completed. (Joe Lawder.)

Sellers Cash Store was one of the first and most essential businesses in the new town of Bakersburg. (Joe Lawder.)

Customers are pictured at Sellers Cash Store, where advertising did pay off to get new customers, especially when it was ten miles to the nearest other town by horse and buggy. (Joe Lawder.)

A young lady, perhaps a potential customer, waits patiently at Sellers Cash Store. (Joe Lawder.)

Pictured here is the lumberyard at Bakersburg. The lumber supplies for the new town came in on the new railroad. (Joe Lawder.)

Grain is delivered from Ochiltree County, Texas, via the railroad at Texhoma. (NMLHS.)

The Adams School was established in 1930 when a number of small districts consolidated after the railroad was built in 1929. A new structure for the school was erected in the new town. In 1950, another new building was constructed, and a gymnasium was added on. The name "Adams" had been proposed for the new Hardesty, but when the old Hardesty townspeople protested, Adams was relegated to the new town on the CRI&P line. By 1929, the new town had grain elevators, general stores, and houses. However, in the 1970s, when the railroad no longer ran through the town, it dwindled to a shadow of its former self, and its school had become a part of Hardesty and Turpin Districts. (Bernell Richards.)

The Steel & Patton Grain Dealers facility in Baker was critical in the delivery of new crops. (Joe Lawder.)

Christine Hitch is an example of those brave women who came west to tame this country, along with their husbands.

This view of the Hitch Ranch House is evidence of the success of the Hitch family, but it is also indicative of many pioneers who tamed this land. (Hitch family archives.)

Six

Early Day Houses and Architecture

Early pioneers of Texas County had very few choices of building materials to work with. Only a few trees were along the rivers and creeks, and nothing was on higher ground. Half dugouts were built, followed by sod houses. Half dugouts were produced below ground level or into a bank. Sod houses were made up of layers of sod cut from the plains, with the blocks of sod stacked on top of each other. Water was carried from the nearest source. If the settlers were extremely lucky, they lived near a creek, river, or pond.

In a few places in the county, there were rock outcroppings that could be cut and used as building material. One place for this kind of material was southeast of Hardesty, and the old Green Ranch house was an example. In some places, there were enough small rocks that could be used, and the Two Sisters houses were of this type. Later, adobe bricks were used in building. Adobe is dirt mixed with straw, formed into a mold, and then dried. This makes it stronger than plain sod because the straw becomes a binder.

Later, freight wagons and the railroads hauled in cut lumber and bricks for the more normal dwellings of the time; these materials greatly increased the size and complexity of design.

Although some of the prominent ranchers erected elegant homes when times were good, it was not until soon after World War II, when veterans returned to establish homes, that a construction boom occurred. Even then, homes tended to be modest and built to similar plans.

In the early 1980s, more elegant houses were built by the prosperous, with the 1990s bringing even more such homes into Texas County.

The more recent Miller Ranch corral uses a stock tank instead of relying on earlier means of creeks, ponds, or the river for watering cattle. (Charles Dean Miller.)

Sod houses were probably the most common type of house built in early Texas County. This was because of the availability of this material. This sod house, located northwest of Guymon, is unique because it features a basement. (Dr. Harold Kachel.)

Pictured here is a stone house built from nearly field rocks in Texas County. These houses do not show any form of secondary work. (Dr. Harold Kachel.)

Seen here is the Wallace Barnes house. The main house was the stone part, with a wooden frame room later added. Notice that some of the rocks used in this structure seem to have had some secondary shaping to make them fit better. This house is situated east of Hardesty. (NMLHS.)

This is one of the Two Sisters houses, built for Boston-born Edna and Emanuella McGrath by their father. These rocks show that they were shaped more than just field rocks, which were used as-is. This house was located northeast of Guymon along the Beaver River. (Dr. Harold Kachel.)

With the Myers Ranch house, a more modern use of rocks and perhaps plaster or stucco of some sort was employed. Stucco is a form of sand and cement applied wet to help seal cracks and weatherproof the building. The old Myers Ranch house was near the Beaver River in Texas County. (NMLHS.)

The old Pafford home, located southeast of Hardesty, may be made of quarried rock like the old Green Ranch house (since it is in the same area) or just square blocks. (NMLHS.)

This old house, which once belonged to Linc Ewing, was built near the riverbank and may have been constructed of quarried rock from that area. There is evidence that several buildings were made from the rock quarry northeast of Hardesty. (NMLHS.)

This place, once the home of Bill Brown, was called the 101 Ranch House. (NMLHS.)

Pictured here is the Etter house, among the first of the formally constructed homes in the area. The new railroad in Texas County during this time was probably the reason for the availability of cut lumber. This house was located south of Hardesty. Notice the very unusual large window on the corner of the house. This was the beginning of the use of picture windows. (NMLHS.)

Pictured here is the Darnell family home, located near the old Pafford home. This house is built of decorative-cut concrete blocks. This pattern was popular among homebuilders of the early 1900s. (NMLHS.)

This painting of the James Cator homestead is by artist Gwenfred Lackey. (NMLHS.)

Seen here is the farmhouse of A. Lawder, located near Tyrone. This frame house and its front porch were typical of farmhouses during the first half of the 20th century. (Joe Lawder.)

The Hitch Ranch buildings and corrals are pictured here. James K. Hitch settled in 1885 and was the first rancher on Coldwater Creek in No Man's Land. (Hitch family archives.)

This elegant early house, built in 1907 at 510 North Academy Street in Guymon, is home to the Louis Latham family. In 1907, this home was quite the showplace. Louis Latham, grandson of the first Louis Latham, and his wife, Sandy, now live in the house, carrying on the Latham tradition of early pioneer merchants and citizens. (Tyler and Geraldine Latham.)

This is an early painting of the house at the Stanley C. Tyler homestead by Gwenfred Lackey. (Tyler and Geraldine Latham.)

Clay Miller stands in front of a rock house that still stands on the Miller Ranch today. (Charles Dean Miller.)

Seven

RAILROADS, IRRIGATION, CORPORATE FARMING, AND FEEDLOTS

By the time the final years of the 1960s came around, several farming methods were changing within Texas County. Flood irrigation became a success. The deepwater source of the Ogallala had been found and was being pumped by large motors running night and day.

The flood system was replaced with large circle units, some running a mile long. The chisel plow, sweep, and strip-farming methods were now providing new methods of working the ground. Minimum-till and chemicals were used to keep more of the foliage on top of the ground; now, no-till, with only chemicals being used to kill unwanted weeds, as well as self-driven GPS-controlled machines, are in the fields.

In addition, research into new varieties of wheat, sorghum, canola, and other crops was conducted by Oklahoma State University at the OSU Research Station at Oklahoma Panhandle State University outside of Goodwell. These varieties are better suited to the dry climate, periodic droughts, and the insects and other predators in the area.

The 1970s also brought an increase in irrigation of crops, counteracting the cyclical droughts of the 1930s, the 1950s, and into the 21st century. Although some curtailing of water use has protected the Ogallala aquifer, irrigation is still used in many large fields, and huge delivery systems are seen throughout Texas County.

The BM&E railroad made it into Bakersburg on July 15, 1926. It was reported by the editor of the *Hooker Advance* that in August of that year, the railroad shipped 65 carloads of wheat from Bakersburg. However, none of these crops would have been marketed had it not been for the coming of the railroads in the early 20th century. Before that, cattle and crops had to be hauled to Liberal, Kansas, or towns adjacent to Texas County in the state of Texas. Markets for Texas County products have been developed through the years with the coming of the first feedlots established by Ladd Hitch and by CFI. The cattle feedlots also brought Swift Packing Company, which built a slaughterhouse along Highway 54 east of Guymon. Although it later closed, it brought jobs and new people to work in the Guymon facility, and the plant building remained there to attract future companies. In the 1930s, as an effort to conserve water and prevent another Dust Bowl as well as to provide jobs during the Dust Bowl and Great Depression, the building of a dam at the juncture of the Beaver River and Coldwater Creek was approved, although actual construction was not begun until the 1970s. The dam was built, but it has seen only trickles of water and the project has been abandoned. However, the majority of projects and efforts to bring prosperity to Texas County have succeeded, and the area has grown in both population and economic well-being. (Sue Weissinger.)

These are railroad cars of the Missouri-Kansas-Texas Railroad (MKT), usually called the Katy Railroad, at Bakersburg. The MKT acquisition of the BM&E was finally completed in July 1931 after many tries. (NMLHS.)

The early elevator and storage facilities at Bakersburg were added as the railroad came into town on July 15, 1926. The town already had the Sellers Grocery Store, a church, and two other businesses. (Dr. Harold Kachel.)

These modern-looking elevators stand along what used to be the Katy Railroad; they are located west of Baker. Unfortunately, like most small towns and elevators, when railroads stop doing business, the towns also go out of business. (Dr. Harold Kachel.)

A lone elevator stands on the east side of the section line of what was to eventually become the town of Mouser; however, the Mouser town plots did not develop. When the Katy Railroad stopped operation, so did this elevator, and it now stands lonely on the prairie by itself. (Dr. Harold Kachel.)

Pictured is a train wreck in the late 1950s on the Rock Island Railroad, formerly known as the Chicago, Rock Island, and Pacific (CRI&P), near Goodwell. A similar wreck occurred in 2012. (Dr. Harold Kachel.)

In this photograph are Dr. Marvin McKee, president of Oklahoma Panhandle State College, and Sen. Leon Fields of Texhoma at the opening dedication of Optima Lake east of Guymon on the Beaver River. The opening day of the dam site was in 1976. (Dr. Harold Kachel.)

Seen here is Optima Lake, built just below the conjunction of the Beaver River and Coldwater Creek in Texas County. This flood control dam was approved by Congress in 1935. It took 41 years of haggling to finally get the project under construction. (Dr. Harold Kachel.)

Pictured is the Optima Dam under construction in the early 1970s. It is supposed to be the longest and highest dam of this type of material and construction known. It is said to be composed of a special mixture of dirt and cement. In this 1974 photograph, the locks and spillway are near completion. (Dr. Harold Kachel.)

In this image, the Optima Dam is completed and shown with about as much water as it has ever had. The dam was finished in 1976, some 40 years after it was approved. The gates are closed in this 2012 photograph, and neither the Beaver River nor Coldwater Creek have run any water into the dam so far. The US Army Corps of Engineers of the Tulsa district has abandoned this project. (Dr. Harold Kachel.)

As farmhouses were improved, they finally got running water. The most common method of getting pressure to the water supply was putting a large tank on top of the well house. Some of these tanks were enclosed, but this one was left in the open with a top on the tank. (Dr. Harold Kachel.)

Tri-County Electric headquarters office is on Gladyas Street in Hooker, as it has been since it was constructed. (JuliAnn Graham of TCEC.)

A Tri-County worker gigs and places one of the high line poles. This was the method of digging pole holes in the 1950s. (JuliAnn Graham of TCEC.)

Tri-County workers install a transformer behind the TCEC office in 1962. As Texas County looks back at its history, the residents realize that one of the most important events in the 20th century in the county was the coming of electricity to both rural farming and ranching areas as well as to the towns. Without that improvement, farms would not have survived in many cases. Electricity provided for the use of new inventions for raising livestock, for irrigation wells, and for running households. It provided for computers for better bookkeeping, for rural students to perform better schoolwork, and for lighting on isolated farms and ranches. Tri-County Electric Cooperative was incorporated on August 15, 1945, by nine founding members. The original members were Orlan Bell of Gray, W.M. Delk of Balko, John R. King of Dombey, Rellis Loring of Hooker, J.S. Houston of Dombey, W.E. Deputy of Hooker, Russell McDaniel of Felt, Raymond Thompson of Boise City, and Ward Hanes of Keyes. The company began with customers in Hooker, where the cooperative office is located, but now includes the entire Oklahoma Panhandle as well as service territory in Texas and Kansas. Today, Tri-County Electric Cooperative has more than 12,000 members, about 23,000 meters, and more than 5,000 miles of line. Texas County is cognizant that without this electrical service, hog farms, feedlots, and packinghouses would not have come to the county. The cooperative is in the process of petitioning to change its name to No Man's Electric Cooperative so as not to be confused with other cooperatives throughout the country. (JuliAnn Graham of TCEC.)

Note the newer substation equipment pictured here at the Tucker Substation near Guymon, built in 2009. (JuliAnn Graham of TCEC.)

A farmer watches a driller prepare an irrigation well on his farm. With the coming of electricity to farms, irrigation would become easier and less expensive, helping farmers deal with the recurring drought seasons. (Dr. Harold Kachel.)

A farmer watches the water pour out of the finished well, a major accomplishment in 1936, still in the Dust Bowl. (Dr. Harold Kechel.)

The other important addition to Texas County, as well as to the entire Panhandle region, was the coming of Panhandle Telephone Cooperative Inc. in 1951. The first meeting of those interested in forming a telephone cooperative was held, and boundaries were established. The first charter was granted in 1955 and the first loan acquired in 1956. The first four exchanges were Adams, Balko, Floris, and Tyrone, two of which were in Texas County. Hardesty and Eva were acquired in 1960–1961, and in 1983, Hooker was added. Today, the cooperative serves the entire Panhandle along with areas in Texas and Kansas. It also was a pioneer in joining Share-Ed Video as the first in the nation to provide ITV so that rural students and teachers could have the same education privileges as the large schools downstate. Those first four schools were the Beaver County High Schools; it now serves all schools in the Panhandle that wish to join. In 2010, the cooperative had $9 million in payroll and paid nearly $10 million in property taxes. It also had 14,062 access lines and served 4,741 customers. Communication in today's high tech world would not be possible without such a service for farms, towns, ranches, schools, and businesses. (Chris Purdy of PTCI.)

One of the first logos of Panhandle Telephone Cooperative Inc. shows how far telephone technology has come to today's multipurpose "can't-live-without" phones. (Stephanie Chapman of PTCI.)

Above, a forklift operator in the PTCI warehouse moves equipment for delivery to the field. Below, a splicer at PTCI keeps connections working. (Both, Chapman, PTCI.)

With the coming of technology and irrigation, both farming and ranching became easier and more profitable. The view of the Herefords in the corral is evidence of quality beef herds being produced on many Texas County ranches. (Freeman.)

Henry C. Hitch is standing beside the meat display of Panhandle A&M College during the Texas County Fair. Since he was one of the leading beef producers in the area and surrounding states, it was appropriate that he be part of the exhibit. (Hitch family archives.)

Eight

Texas County Today

Texas County is vastly different today from the early days when it was mostly ranches, then small farms established by homesteaders. The county is mostly level plains and a few rolling hills formed by the Beaver River and its tributaries. Circle irrigation and mile-long irrigation systems provide equipment that makes the county one of the most productive agricultural counties in several categories in the nation. Today, the ranches use technology and the latest methods of raising cattle. The county also ranks high in natural gas and petroleum production, sitting on one of the largest natural gas formations in the world. In addition, Texas County has been able to attract businesses related to these natural resources, with a large hog production company and its related hog-raising farms, as well as pipelines, gathering stations, and other petroleum entities. The county has built modern, quality schools to educate its children for life. Most importantly, of course, is the progress its citizens have made in these areas, as they are always looking toward the future while maintaining a respect for and knowledge of those brave souls who came before.

The Coots gas well is being drilled in this 1928 photograph. This is not much of a rig compared to the ones now drilling deep and/or horizontal wells. (NMLHS.)

Pictured here is the Hurlimann no. 1 gas well in 1926. Oil and gas came early to Texas County compared to the rest of the Panhandle. It still remains one of the top producers of gas in the state, and Texas County has the advantage of sitting above the large Hugoton Gas Field. (NMLHS.)

When the Seaboard Farms and Packing House came to Texas County, as well as surrounding areas in 1995, hog operations were greatly expanded. Seaboard is one of the largest employers in the county. Gerald Dixon stands beside the nursery unit, one of the many run by Seaboard. (Gerald Dixon.)

The four Dixon brothers stand beside Gerald Dixon's Cessna 210 Turbo after a flight over the area. From left to right are Ernest, Gerald, Oral, and John Dixon. Gerald has been flying for over 50 years. Airplanes have enabled businesspeople to be more efficient since the Panhandle is so far from the capital or any large city. (Gerald Dixon.)

Pictured here is the Texhoma, Oklahoma, elevator as it stands today. Texhoma is fortunate to still have a main railroad running through the town so that it can still shop grain, an advantage that most towns in the Panhandle are unable to take advantage of now. (Dr. Harold Kachel.)

The No Man's Land Museum is operated by the No Man's Land Historical Society, which was founded October 3, 1934, by a group of Oklahoma Panhandle residents who were interested in preserving the uniqueness of the area. The museum is located in Goodwell, adjacent to the campus of Oklahoma Panhandle State University. The museum board of directors, who oversee museum operations, represent the three Panhandle counties. (NMLHS.)

The Museum Club of PAMC was organized on April 5, 1932. Dr. Claude Fly established the club on the second floor of the Sewell-Loofbourrow building, and it moved several times before the No Man's Land Museum was built in 1950. The club was a means of educating students through field trips to surrounding areas, even as far as Arizona, as well as through activities such as the relay race from Kansas to Texas through the Panhandle. The Museum Club was very active until it disbanded in 1971 during the college presidency of Dr. Tom Palmer. (Dr. Harold Kachel.)

Gerald Dixon, president of the No Man's Land Historical Society, receives a plaque in appreciation for the society's publication of Fred Tracy's book *Recollections of No Man's Land*. The state award is from the Oklahoma Heritage Foundation. Others in the picture are members of the board of NMLHS and museum manager Sue Weissinger. They are, from left to right, (first row) Jay Stanfield; Sue Weissinger; editor Pauline Hodges; Gerald Dixon; and David Bryant, president of Oklahoma Panhandle State University; (second row) Ron Kincannon, president of NMLHS; Paul Hitch; Stephen Long; and Doug Dale. (Gerald Dixon.)

Texas County can celebrate all the progress in farming since the days when broomcorn was the major crop at the beginning of the 20th century. (NMLHS.)

Thanks to modern technology and education, the Bennet Ranch operation near Texhoma is an example of how far raising cattle has come from those early trail herds and ranches in 1886. (NMLHS.)

Semitrucks now haul grain from field to elevator to railroads in a fraction of the time these men spent just getting their grain to market in Texhoma in the early 1900s. (NMLHS.)

During drought years, residents in Texas County are reminded of how much farming methods have improved from the great plow-up that led to the Dust Bowl. A major factor in these improvements has been the development over the last 75 years of better and more efficient equipment, such as this circular plow, photographed in the 1960s. (NMLHS.)

The depot at Tyrone, pictured in the 1950s, serves as a reminder that much has been written about railroads. However, residents in Texas County, as well as the entire region, should remember that without the coming of the railroads to No Man's Land, modern farming and shipping of cattle would have been impossible.

This is all that is left of the towns of Beulah and Muncy, as the railroads failed to fulfill their promise of building west through Texas County. (NMLHS.)

Windmills such as these are fast disappearing in Texas County. They were power sources for water on the farms and ranches for many years and are now being replaced by submergible pumps and solar panels. They serve as reminders of how far farming, ranching, and other businesses, as well as life in general, in Texas County have come in the last 100-plus years. (Dr. Harold Kachel.)

Pictured here are Colonel and Mrs. Norman Wilmeth, whose family (the Dixons) are from those early, hearty settlers who came to an untamed land to survive and thrive. Colonel Wilmeth graduated from Guymon High School in 1938, spent years in the Air Force as a glider pilot in World War II, then returned to Guymon to become successful in real estate, as an auctioneer, and as an active member in civic affairs. His wife has been his cheerleader, his helper, and his inspiration. They are typical of what has made Texas County so great. (Gerald Dixon.)

www.ingramcontent.com/pod-product-compliance
Lightning Source LLC
LaVergne TN
LVHW081338110826
845153LV00010B/400

* 9 7 8 1 5 3 1 6 6 1 3 1 1 *